TRACK AND FIELD
RULES IN PICTURES

Michael Brown

Book Consultant: Don Kavadas,
National Chairman, Regional Director, Amateur Athletic Union

A Perigee Book

Perigee Books
are published by
The Putnam Publishing Group
200 Madison Avenue
New York, NY 10016

Library of Congress Cataloging-in-Publication Data

Brown, Michael, date.
    Track and field rules in pictures / Michael Brown; book
consultant, Don Kavadas.
        p.   cm.
    ''A Perigee book.''
    ISBN 0-399-51620-4
    1. Track-athletics—Rules.   I. Kavadas, Don.   II. Title.
GV1060.67.B76   1990   89-49194 CIP
796.42—dc20

Printed in the United States of America

1   2   3   4   5   6   7   8   9   10

This book has been printed on acid-free paper.
                ∞

CONTENTS

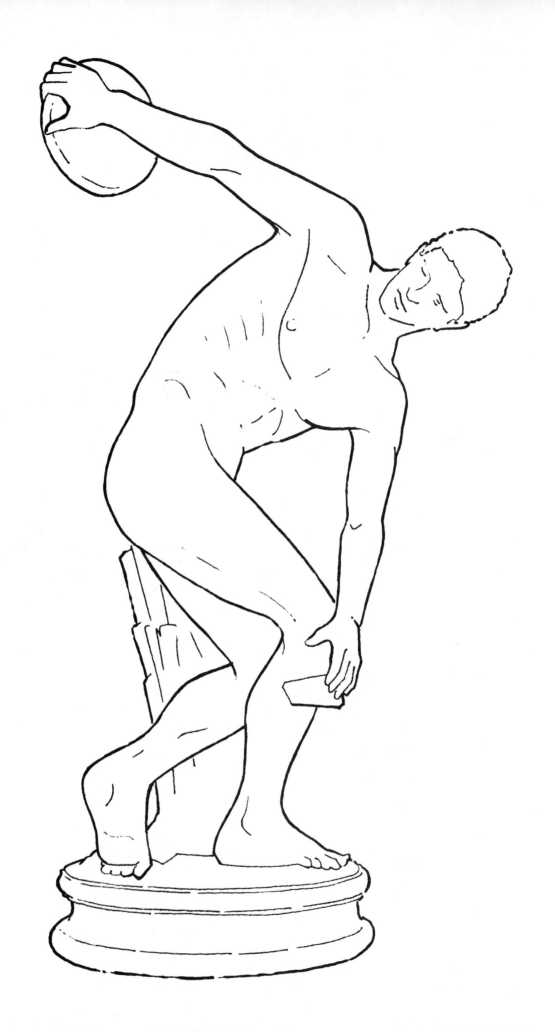

INTRODUCTION

Track and field, the oldest of organized sporting events, is not a single sport, but a collection of related running, jumping, and throwing events. This may be why, although various attempts have been made through the years to professionalize track and field, it has largely remained an amateur endeavor. It also has remained more closely associated with Olympics than other big-time, big-money professional and collegiate sports.

The origins of modern track and field reach back to the Olympics of ancient Greece. Formal records of those events exist from about A.D. 400, but we know they existed long before that, because Greek artists had been portraying the games in sculpture and on the surfaces of pottery for centuries. As time wore on, running, jumping, and throwing competitions were held less frequently. The early Christian Romans banned what they viewed as the pagan Olympics. In the Middle Ages and Renaissance, recreational athletics were actually forbidden by the monarchs and other rulers in favor of archery and other more warlike practices.

Track and field events as we know them have a more recent ancestor in the rural competitions of early-nineteenth-century Scotland and England. Those early competitions among unlettered rural athletes gained popularity partly because working people in England were not serfs. A growing middle class, who enjoyed the benefits of space, time and numerous public holidays, also helped bring track and field competitions back into popularity. These country games thrived a century before the prewar, white-clad gentlemen of sports portrayed in such movies as *Chariots of Fire.*

It was not until near the end of the nineteenth century that so many of the track and especially field events appeared—after being borrowed, transported, and in many cases transformed from their rural cousins—on the athletic fields of England's upper-class public schools. By the mid to late nineteenth century, England and Scotland were conducting numerous, disparate track and field–based athletic events, among them the Highland Games. In 1880, the universities of Oxford and Cambridge organized these all into the Amateur Athletic Association.

During this time, a century-long wave of emigration helped to export track and field events to the United States. Early intercontinental competitions were also taking place, some of them quite unusual: In 1862, the American Indian Louis "Deerfoot" Bennett visited England to race Jack White, a.k.a. the Gateshead Clipper. White won, breaking for the first time the 30-minute mark for a 6-mile run; eight years earlier, Deerfoot had set a record for the 12-mile run at 1 hour, 2½ minutes. Both of these records stood until the 1920s. After 1920, almost everything in organized track and field endeavors changed.

Athletic events similar to those in England, Scotland, and the United States also were developing throughout Europe during the nineteenth century, leading inevitably to the first Olympics of 1896 in Athens. However, a more full-scale international meet had taken place the previous year in New York between the London and the New York Athletic Clubs. Apparently up until then, the British had considered the Americans to be amateur amateurs, but that belief died on Travers Island, New York: The visitors from England were thoroughly routed.

Various Olympics were held between 1896 and 1912 in the United States and abroad, but it wasn't until 1912 in Stockholm that the Olympics, and by extension, track and field athletics started to grow into their own and gain a world-acknowledged stature. A year after the successful and well-organized Stockholm games, the International Amateur Athletic Federation was formed and it formally laid down which events were to constitute future Olympics. From this point, the evolution of track and field events into the form we practice today raced forward.

Women were not included until 1928, only a handful of countries participated, and the participants still tended to be middle-class college boys. Indeed, not until 1936, when the

Germans sent a well-trained, rigorously prepared team did the games forever lose the atmosphere of "gentlemen sporting on a Sunday afternoon." During the years of World War II the Olympics were not held. Then, after that hiatus and at the onset of the Cold War, the Soviets sent to the 1952 Olympics a fierce, well-trained team. In the following decade, athletics were but one area in which the United States and USSR were to compete hotly, and partly as a result, track and field events, techniques, and training methods evolved more than ever before in their history. The Olympics reached a new peak in 1960 with the first worldwide televising of the games.

Contemporary athletics have become highly standardized. The program is much different than it was either in Greece or in the country fields of machine-age England. In terms of equipment, technique, and training, even a 1920s competitor would be lost in today's arena. The discus, javelin, hammer, tracks, and landing pits all have undergone transformation. The changes just since 1960 include the first flexible fiberglass poles, the first foam landing area, and the first synthetic track. The javelin, hammer, and discus have not only been redesigned, but made of new materials; and the methods of measuring and timing have become an exact science that electronically measures fractions of seconds and of millimeters.

One thing at least remains the same. The heart of these racing, running, jumping, and hurling events—even at the international level—is intact. The focus remains, and must remain, on one individual's ability to train, practice, and compete.

The Governing Bodies

The International Amateur Athletic Federation (IAAF) is the international governing body of track and field. This organization regulates these sports worldwide and helps coordinate the Olympics, the Pan-American Games, the Commonwealth Games, and other events of international importance. The United States affiliate of the IAAF is The Athletics Congress of the United States (TAC). These two organizations have some minor differences in rules; for instance, the IAAF does not recognize indoor records, while TAC does. TAC was formed in 1979 to help resolve differences between AAU and the NCAA, two much older bodies. The NCAA concerns itself with college-level athletics, the AAU with amateur athletes of all ages, in or out of school. Also, the National Federation of State High School Athletics Association (NFSHSAA) concerns itself with high school sports. All of these organizations vary their track and field regulations slightly, and both the NFSHSAA and the NCAA have slightly different rules in order to accommodate their age groups and educational mission.

One rather confusing current situation concerns metric (meters) versus imperial (feet and inches) systems of measurements. In the United States we tend to use feet and inches; however, the Olympic trials are conducted in meters. In this volume we have described the events primarily in meters—the way they are referred to worldwide. In describing equipment and competition area for field events (such as the throwing circle for the discus) we have used feet and inches, which are more familiar to our readers.

Another important and noticeable difference is that indoor and outdoor events vary quite a bit. The indoor season is winter, rather than summer. Races often are run on smaller, banked tracks, many of the throwing events are not practiced indoors, and some of the distances in the races are different. Most of these differences have been caused by the limitations imposed by the size of the indoor arena, and therefore a whole different set of records is kept for indoor athletics. Despite these differences, it's important to remember that these indoor or outdoor track and field games are spiritual siblings, just as American Leaguers and National Leaguers are both playing baseball.

REGISTRATION

All those athletes and teams hoping to compete in official TAC events must be registered beforehand. Once a competitor has registered to compete and arrived at the meet, he or she may be in for a jolt: More than many sporting events, the precompetition activities of track and field are quite chaotic for the initiate—especially larger TAC-sponsored events. There are many officials moving about, distributing numbers to be worn, checking equipment, registering and measuring the competition areas, and in general overseeing a highly organized, staggered set of competitions that might last for several days. If the meet is outdoors, there might be the weather to worry about, and if it's indoors the din of the pregame hubbub would make an orchestra warm-up sound like soothing music.

The Athletic Congress of the United States is divided into senior and junior classes. The minimum age for senior and junior events for both women's and men's events is 14, with one exception: men's senior long-distance runners must be 16. Competitors older than 20 must compete as seniors. All associations within The Athletic Congress (TAC) of the United States adhere to these divisions. TAC and the AAU hold championship competitions in track events, field events, long-distance running, and race walking. The competitions are held first at the association level, then regionals, then nationals.

Youth athletics programs generally include track, field, race-walking, cross-country, and multi-event competitions. The program is divided into five female and five male divisions. The age divisions are: bantam, 10 and younger; midget, 11–12; youth or junior, 13–14; intermediate, 15–16; and young men's/women's, 18 and up. The ages are approximate, because it's the competitor's year of birth that determines his or her division. For instance, 1990's bantam competitors are all born in 1980. There are also many masters or seniors age groups for athletes 35–39, 40–44, and up; for most events the grouping is in five-year age groups. In addition, there are special adaptations of the rules for the United States Cerebral Palsy Athletic Association, the National Wheelchair Athletic Association (including chair specifications), the Special Olympics, and for the United States Association for Blind Athletes.

As much as possible, the rules set down by The Athletics Congress for championship competitions are used to conduct all track and field events. Rules may vary in procedures for conducting meets.

In preparing to compete, athletes should remember that decorum is also covered by the rules. It's against the rules to undress anywhere except in the changing rooms—this doesn't include donning and doffing warm-up suits. When dressed, clothing should be clean and not indecently revealing. Competitors also should not dress themselves in getups that make it hard for the judges to make decisions. All competitors must wear shirts. The AAU insists that younger competitors wear foot coverings, not necessarily shoes.

As for shoes, competitors may wear two of them, one—high jumpers sometimes compete wearing only one shoe—or none at all. They can be similarly creative with the use of socks. Any shoes worn, however, must not be specially rigged for extra assistance—no jets or springs or bat wings. Also, a single shoe may have no more than 11 spike positions and a competitor may not use more than 11 spikes per shoe. The maximum legal length of spikes varies from event to event. Grooves and ridges on the soles of the shoes are okay, so long as they're made of basically the same material as the sole itself. In the high jump, the sole may be no thicker than one-half inch and the heel no thicker than three-quarters of an inch.

Competitors must wear their numbers conspicuously when competing, and they may not cut or fold them. If only one number is provided, it is worn on the back; two, on the chest and back. Sometimes when photo-finish equipment is used, competitors will need to have numbers on the sides of their shorts.

In pole vault and high jump, numbers need only be worn on either front or back. Numbers must be worn on front—and should be worn on the back, too—for cross country, long distance, and race walks. The number especially needs to be visible at all check points and at the finish line.

Finally, and most seriously, no drugs. Using any substance or stimulant to increase the power, action, performance, or mental condition of the athlete before or during competition is forbidden.

RUNNING EVENTS

In the ancient games of Greece, there were only three running events: a sprint, a medium-length race, and a long-distance run. Today we have the sprints, which are all-out power races; the relay races, requiring teamwork and precision timing to pass a baton; the hurdles, demanding both speed and phenomenal timing; mid-distance running, which calls on speed, technique, endurance, and strategy; the marathon, that singular feat of superhuman endurance that pits runners not only against each other but themselves; the steeplechase, a high-speed obstacle course; and race walking, a combination of speed and control.

The standard oval track has at least 6 lanes and a circumference of approximately 400 meters. The inside lane is called the pole and it is the most popular lane for longer-distance runs. The preferred paving material over the last twenty years has been synthetic rubber.

The following is the general breakdown of running events for junior and senior participants:

OUTDOOR	INDOOR
Men's Events	
100-meter dash	55- or 60-meter dash
200-meter dash	400-meter dash
400-meter dash	500-meter run
800-meter run	800-meter and 1000-meter runs
1500-meter run	1500-meter or 1-mile run
5000-meter run	3000-meter run
10,000-meter run	5000-meter run
20,000-meter walk	55- or 60-meter high hurdles
110-meter high hurdles	various relays
400-meter hurdles	
3000-meter steeplechase	
400-, 1600-, and 3200-meter relay (4 x 800)	
Women's Events	
100-meter dash	55- or 60-meter dash
200-meter dash	200-meter dash
400-meter dash	400-meter dash
800-meter run	800- and 1000-meter run
1500-meter run	1500-meter or 1-mile run
3000-meter run	3000-meter run
5000-meter run	55- or 60-meter hurdles
10,000-meter run	various relays
10,000-meter walk	
100-meter hurdles	
400-meter hurdles	
400-meter relay (4 × 100)	
1600-meter relay (4 × 400)	
3200-meter relay (4 × 800)	

TRIAL
HEATS

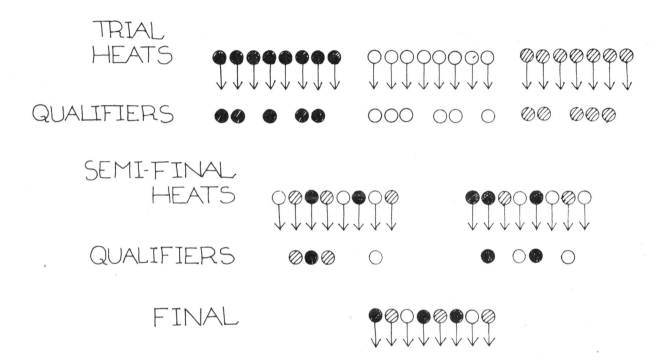

QUALIFIERS

SEMI-FINAL
HEATS

QUALIFIERS

FINAL

If there are more runners entered into an event than the number of lanes on the track, then a series of competitions leading up to the final contest will be held. These are called heats and are organized like this: All the contestants are assigned to a preliminary race. At least three runners from each of these preliminary races will move on to the next semifinal heat.

Seeding is done in semifinal heats so that the fastest runners are spread out among all the heats and do not eliminate each other at the onset. When forming heats, the runners are seeded first according to place, next according to time.

In all running events, no one is allowed to mark up the running surface or the area outside it—except in relay races, where a runner may leave a small marker in his or her lane for the incoming teammate, to guide them to the proper lane for the actual relay.

At the Starting Line

All competitors must be behind the starting line—not touching it or the surface in front of it with hands or feet. Longer races begin with a standing start.

Shorter races begin with a crouch start. When starting in a crouch, both hands must be touching the track in the "set" position. For races and relay legs of 440 yards and less, the crouch start must be used unless the racer is prevented from doing so by a permanent physical disability.

Starting blocks are mandatory for the races where the crouch start is mandatory. They're used so the runner may push off, and to protect the track. Runners may not push off from the blocks with their hands. Starting blocks must be made of rigid material; they may not have any spring or coil to aid the runner. They should be easy to handle so they can be moved quickly. Starting blocks may not be used for any race longer than 440 meters.

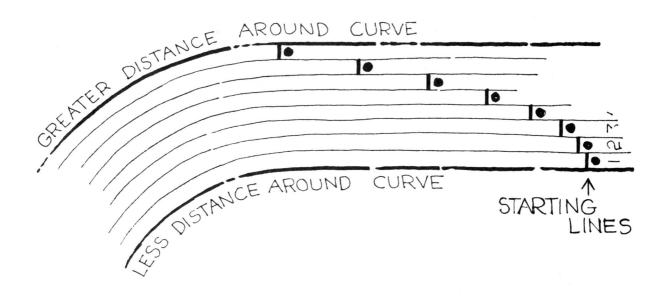

In the longer races such as the 800 meters that go around turns, the starting line is curved. This assures that the runner racing around the outside of the track (who runs a much greater distance around the curves than competitors on the inside of the track) will, by the time he reaches the finish line, have run the same distance as everyone else. No matter what lane the runners start in, all of them will have started the same distance from the finish line.

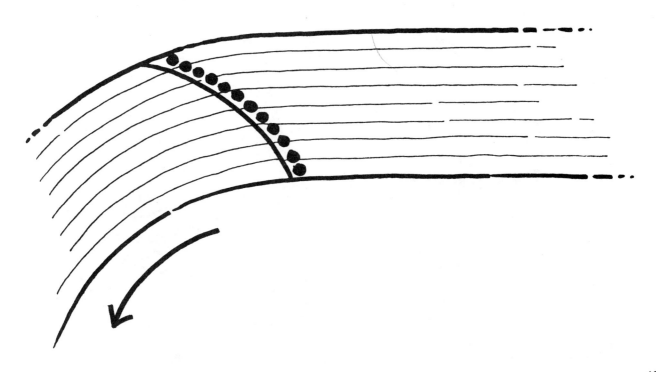

Prior to the starting gun, the starter uses the following commands: "On your mark" and "set." For outdoor races of 440 yards or more and indoor races of 600 yards or more, the starter says only "On your mark" and then fires the gun.

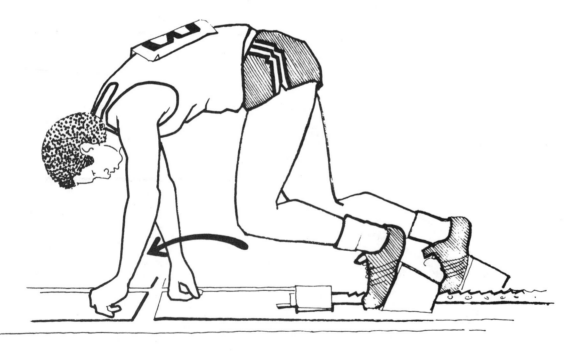

A false start occurs when a runner is on the mark, and then leaves his mark with hand or foot before the shot.

If a racer disturbs the other competitors after the starter has called out "On your mark," a false start will be called on that competitor.

Also, when the competitors hear the starter's "set" command, they must assume a set position. If one of them fails to do this in a reasonable time, a false start will be called.

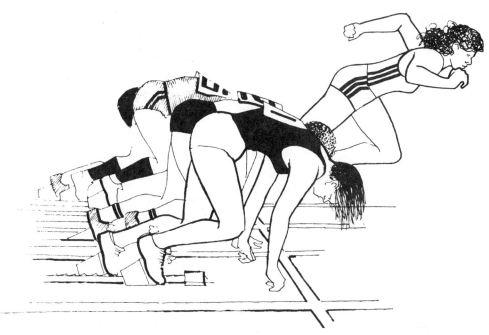

If the starter or recall starter considers a start to be unfair, he or she recalls the racers by refiring the pistol. If this is done because a racer "beat the gun," a false start is called on the offender.

When every runner is in the proper standing or crouching position, the pistol is fired to start the race.

A competitor who commits a false start is excused the first time, but disqualified the second time. If the starter needs to warn the competitors or has any cause for concern after the commands are begun, the starter may order the competitors to "stand up" and leave their ready positions.

Running in Lanes

The race is on—the crowd is cheering, the runners are straining to push themselves to the limit or pacing themselves for the long haul. Each race calls for different strategies, and different races have different rules regarding how much of the race the runners must run in their original lanes. The shorter, more explosive races are the 100-meter, 200-meter, and 400-meter events. In these races, each racer is supposed to have a separate lane at least four feet wide. If this is impossible, the lanes may be as narrow as three feet, but that's the absolute minimum.

How much of a relay race is run entirely in the runner's original lane varies from race to race. The runner in this illustration is waiting in his lane for the baton handoff.

For example, in a 400-meter race, the runners go around the track twice and must stay in their original lanes until the race finishes. In an 800-meter race, a middle-distance race, the runners stay in their own lanes only until the first turn, then they can break out of that formation and move to "the pole." The long-distance events are not run in lanes.

In the shorter races, runners must stick to their original lanes from beginning to end. If the race is longer, it is run only part of the way in lanes. A marker signifies the end of the lane-run portion of the race, after which runners may switch lanes.

Generally, in races run entirely in lanes, runners are not penalized for moving toward the outside of a curved track. This is known as running wide and gives the runner no advantage, since it in fact causes the runner to run a greater distance. However, they will be penalized for crossing the inside boundary, as that shortens the distance they must run. While racing, a runner may step on or over the inside line three times, but will be penalized on the fourth step on or over the lane line.

Only the width of the right-hand line is included when measuring the lane. This runner is not committing a lane violation. Moving to an inside lane may cause disqualification. Moving to an outside lane will not, unless such a movement impedes another runner.

For almost all races the direction of the running will be so that the runners have their left hands to the inside of the track.

Even if his or her feet remain in the lane, a racer may not interfere with another's progress by jostling or deliberately blocking. The offender may and very likely will be disqualified. If such an offense takes place in a heat, the referee can let the mistreated competitor compete in a later round. And furthermore, if in a final race, the referee can either disqualify the offender or demand that the entire race be rerun.

Longer events are not run entirely in lanes. (Longer events are not generally held in youth programs.) For example, the first turn of 800- and 880-meter events are run in lanes and after that runners are free to jockey for position. The 1500-meter runners pictured here are not committing lane violations.

Even if a race is not run in lanes, a competitor must not leave the track or course. If he does, the race is over for that runner, and he may not rejoin the race to run or to assist another competitor.

However, in races of 20,000 meters or more, runners may leave the track, with the permission of an official, but they must take care that their exit and reentry does not shorten their race.

If a racer jostles or interferes with another—even when there are no lane restrictions—the jostler can be disqualified. Above, the runner on the right must be fully and clearly ahead of the runner on the left before moving in front of that runner. He cannot force the trailing runner to break stride.

Runners may not slow down to impede other runners . . .

. . . nor may they force their way through a group of runners.

Assistance

In road races and long-distance walking events, competitors may be assisted in certain ways, which is covered later. During all other race events, any competitor who gets any assistance from anyone, including pacing by another person or by a device, may be disqualified.

If athletes receive advice from people outside the competition area, that's okay, as long as no technological device is used. The athlete is not allowed to have anybody who is not taking part in the competition go with them to the mark or along the course. The competitor also isn't allowed to take assistance or refreshment from anyone during the actual competition without official permission.

An athlete receiving advice or assistance during a race will be cautioned the first time; a second offense results in disqualification.

Hurdles

The informal rural "olympics" of England conducted hurdle events through the end of the nineteenth century, and these competitions were taken up by schools and colleges. The basic setup then and today has remained similar. Relay races are of varying lengths, but they usually have ten hurdles (a flight) evenly spaced in each lane. The height and spacing of the hurdles varies from race to race, just as the race distances do. In earlier versions, however, the hurdles themselves were very firmly planted. The object in those days was to get over this firmly planted barrier somehow, clearing it completely without tripping and breaking one's neck, which could be easily done if one's foot catches on the hurdle. In today's hurdles, the object is to clear the hurdle in a smooth-flowing motion. It's more a matter of fluid-motion run-and-jump speed, grace, and timing, rather than the obstacle course it once was. Hurdle events include, among others, 100 meters and 400 meters.

The top bar of the standard hurdle might be made of wood or light metal. The hurdle is constructed so that a force of just 8 pounds across the top edge of the crossbar will cause it to fall forward. The height of the bar is adjustable.

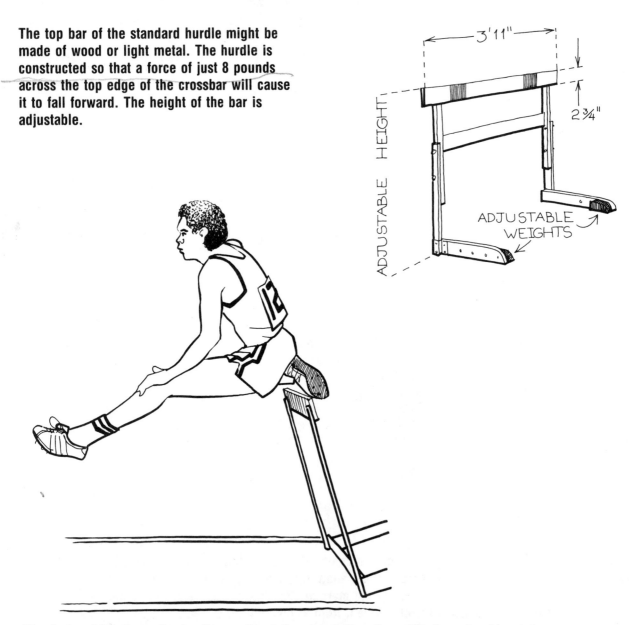

Simply knocking down the hurdle won't get the competitor disqualified or stop him or her from claiming a record, but honest effort must be made to clear all the hurdles. Hitting hurdles actually slows the runners down.

Disqualification may occur if a hurdler trails a foot or leg beside and below the level of the hurdle while clearing, jumps or knocks down a hurdle in another lane, or deliberately (in the referee's opinion) kicks or knocks a hurdle down with a hand.

Steeplechase

The steeplechase is, in comparison with the hurdles, a truer obstacle course. It is probably a descendant of the cross-country races that were held at fairs and carnivals in rural areas, where participants would race from one church or one village to the next as the crow flies. Today's steeplechase, however, doesn't depend on nature (in the form of ditch banks, creeks, and thickets) or civilization (in the form of walls and fences) to provide the obstacles. The steeplechase has been standardized. It is an enclosed course, of a standard length, with a standard number of hurdles at a more-or-less standard distance and construction.

The standard distance of a steeplechase is 3000 meters, which is approximately $1^6/_7$ miles ($7\frac{1}{2}$ laps around the track). It has 28 hurdles and 7 water jumps.

The exact length of the laps and the precise positions of the water jumps and hurdles are not rigidly prescribed. The important thing is that there be enough distance from the start to the first hurdle to prevent the racers from being overcrowded. There also should be about 76 yards from the last jump to the finish.

Each competitor goes over the jumps, and over—or through—the water. If anyone steps to the side of the jump or hurdle, or trails a foot below and to the side of the hurdle while jumping it, he or she will be disqualified. The important thing is to clear the hurdle or jump and pass over the water—it's okay to put a foot on the hurdle itself or land in water.

Relays

In standard relays, four runners on a team each run one 400- or 800-meter leg of a race. Each runner runs one-fourth of the race carrying the baton—a short round stick, measuring 10 to 11 inches and weighing 1¾ ounces. All teams in the race are given letters, A, B, C, and so on, rather than numbers. The baton is passed at the end of the runner's leg of the race to the next racer of that team. In early events—and in playground versions of the sport—runners had only to touch one another. But in regulation competition the baton has been required for such a sufficiently long amount of time that the phrase ''passing the baton'' has entered into popular use as a metaphor for any kind of passing on of responsibility.

Relay demands speed and technique, like any race, but it also has the added fun, excitement, and timing of teamwork. The overall aim is to get the baton around the track as fast as possible, and if there is a single most important element in the race, it is probably the method of passing the baton. In that split second the finishing runner enters the takeover zone to the rear of the outgoing runner, the fresh runner holds one hand behind, takes the baton, and rockets away. It really happens so fast that it is hard to see at normal speed, and any error—stumbling, dropping the baton—costs valuable time and might be devastating to the outcome of the competition for that team.

Relay events usually include the 4 × 100 and the 4 × 400 (four runners going 400 meters each) and sometimes the 4 × 800 race. Interestingly, in 1893 at the University of Pennsylvania, a 40 × 440 was held. That's no typo: For each of the two teams, 40 young men each ran 440 meters.

In the 4 × 400 and 4 × 800 races, the takeover zone is marked by a line drawn across the track 10 meters on either side of the starting line. In the 4 × 100, however, the takeover zone is 20 meters long at 100-yard intervals around the track. This is where the new runner takes the baton from the runner that just came in. If a team member receives or hands off outside this zone, the whole team is disqualified.

In the takeover zone, it's the position of the baton that matters as to whether it's in or out of the takeover zone, not the position of the body or limbs of either runner. The runners in the illustration are passing the baton in the legal takeover zone.

In the shorter relays, it's all right for the relieving runner to begin running in preparation for the handoff. This preparatory run can begin as much as 11 yards before the takeover zone, but no farther than that. The actual passing of the baton must take place in the takeover zone.

Runners must carry the baton by hand. The baton is considered "passed" only when it's in the hand of the receiver. It may not be thrown.

If it's dropped, it must be picked up by the runner who dropped it.

The runner may leave the lane to pick it up, but shouldn't interfere with the other runners in doing so.

After passing the baton a runner is supposed to keep moving along in his or her own lane and avoid interfering with the other teams. Botching up an opponent after passing on the baton could get the team disqualified.

Different races have different rules for when runners may leave their original lanes while moving around the track.

Middle, Long-distance, and Marathon Running

With the resurgence in interest in organized sports, distance running began to gain popularity around 1850. The professional international runner Deerfoot Bennett, mentioned earlier in this book, is from this period. In the modern era, distance running's most noteworthy event was the achievement of the less-than-4-minute mile in 1954 by Roger Bannister. Distance events commonly run today include, among others, the 800- and 1500-meter, the mile, the 3000- and 5000-meter, the 10,000-meter, and, at the college level and above, the marathon.

Marathon popularity is something of a recent phenomenon. It's hard to believe that scarcely a generation ago, marathon racing was looked on by the general public as the province of exercise fanatics. In the last couple of decades this has changed to the point where star marathon runners' names are in the limelight. Not only that, marathons such as those in Boston and New York and in small cities all over the United States have popularized the sport to the point where it's not unusual to see grandparents, wheelchairers, and young kids taking part—and finishing.

It's surprising, therefore, to realize that it wasn't until recently that women ran the marathon in the Olympics. But women have been making rapid improvements in their times for this 26-mile, 385-yard event.

While all long-distance running emphasizes an economy of effort, that consideration finds its extreme expression in marathoning. There are very few bursts of speed, no dramatic leaps, just a steady effort and a reliance on all the runner's reserves of stamina.

It is from marathon racing, by the way, that the expression ''hitting the wall'' of resistance derives. Most runners agree that in this long race, there is a point at about the 20- to 22-mile mark where collapse seems inevitable, and from that point to the finish it is truly an endurance contest against the self.

Middle-distance events such as the 800-meter race or the 1500–3000-meter race are conducted around the track. A long-distance or road-race course takes place on the streets, and roads or paths of grass, gravel, or dirt. Runners in long distance and road racing will be immediately disqualified if the referee or appeal jury finds that they have ''cut the course''—that is, that they have changed the route by shortening it, to gain an advantage.

31

The course itself will be marked so that the runners can keep to it. Each turn or intersection should have a sign to prevent wrong turns, and major intersections are guarded by monitors, who stand at or near the change of direction.

Distance markers are placed beside the course about every 2 to 3 miles.

Runners must stop if a race official or medical staffer tells them to.

Refreshment and sponging stations are set up at regular intervals. In the marathon, the first station is about six miles into the race, and the next ones about every three miles, with water-only stations in between these. Competitors are not supposed to take refreshment anywhere but at official stations; if they do, they can be disqualified.

Race Walking

Race walking has been known to make non–track and field aficionados giggle. *Why are those people WADDLING?* Race walkers can satisfy themselves against this ignorance with the knowledge that race walking is a good deal older and more established as a sport than such Johnny-come-latelys as basketball, and also that it is sport for overall development, including the upper body.

As a recognized sport, race walking has records as early as the seventeenth century, and it has been included in the Olympics since 1908. The distances of the standard race have varied over time: 50 kilometers was the Olympic standard in 1932; later, a 20-kilometer race was added, and this distance ultimately supplanted the 50-kilometer altogether.

An intense, high-speed version of ordinary walking, the vital requirement of race walking is "one foot on the ground at all times."

In the correct race walk one foot stays on the ground at all times and the knee is straight momentarily as it supports the body. This leg needs to be straight only when it is supporting the weight of the body.

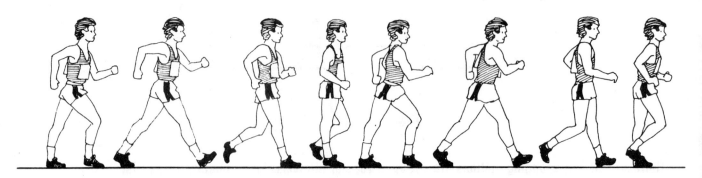

This is not proper race walking, since there is never a moment when the leg is straight, the knee unbent.

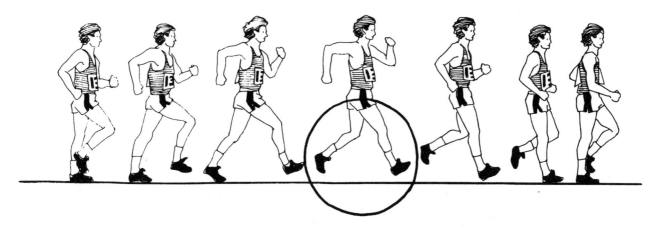

This race walker has not stepped so that contact with the ground is unbroken. The forward foot should have come down and touched the ground before the rear foot leaves it. Each leg must be straight—not bent at the knee—at least momentarily as it is vertical and supporting the body.

The race-walking judges determine whether the walking is fair or unfair. Their rulings are final and can't be appealed. Judges must warn race walkers that they're in danger of violating the definition of race walking, before ruling against them.

In order for a competitor to be disqualified during competition, three walking judges must rule against the competitor's way of walking.

The Finish Line

All running and walking events—even the 26-mile marathon—must end somewhere short of the rainbow, and this somewhere is the finish line. Whether finishing to the roar of thousands at an international meet or just a few clapping hands at a local event, it feels great to be the first one over the line. However, just as in the running of the race itself, there's more involved than just putting one foot quickly in front of the other. There are a few things competitors should keep in mind about the finish line.

In all straightaway races, start and finish lines are painted so that the race distance begins just behind the starting line and extends to just up to the beginning of the finish line. In record-breaking finishes, this distinction can matter. The finish line, drawn across the track or course, should extend out to each finish post.

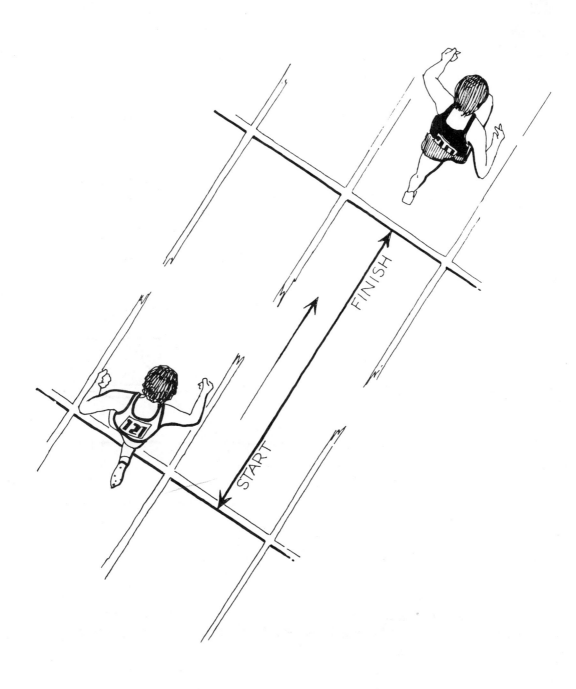

The string stretched from post to post is there to aid the judges—it is not the finish line.

When the string is placed, care should be taken that it is not of a material that might hurt the runner breaking through. Worsted string or thread, or tape, is usually used.

The finishing position and time of the runners is determined by the order that the *body* reaches the finish line. This rule is important and very literal; it means the torso, and not the arms, leg, head, feet, or hands.

When the tie affects who will go on to the next round, the tying racers both continue on. If this is not practical, the tying runners compete again. If the tie is for first place, the referee decides whether the competitors compete again or if the tie stands.

FIELD EVENTS

"Field" events are called that because they take place in specific places out in an open area or in a large indoor area, rather than being run along a track or course. While running is a part of some field events—the running start, for instance—the emphasis is on another type of feat, a jump or throw. More so than running, field events are identified solely as amateur endeavors. This may be exactly the reason why they appeal to some very talented individuals.

The field events are:

Jumps: the long and triple, judged by the distance of the jump; and the high jump and the pole vault, which are judged by height.

Throws: shot put, discus, hammer, and javelin. All these involve throwing an object, in a certain manner, the greatest possible distance. They're judged by the distance of the throw. The general breakdown of field events:

OUTDOOR

Men's Events

High jump
Pole vault
Long jump
Triple jump
Shot put (7.260 Kg)
Discus throw (2 Kg)
Javelin throw (800 G)
Hammer throw (7.260 Kg)

Women's Events

High jump
Long jump
Triple jump
Shot put (4.000 Kg)
Discus throw (2.000 Kg)
Javelin throw (800 Gm)

INDOOR

High jump
Pole vault
Long jump
Triple jump
Shot put (7.260 Kg)
Weight throw (15.875 Kg)

High jump
Long jump
Triple jump
Shot put

General Rules

In field events other than the high jump or pole vault (which are scratch events) (see p. 36), the competitor gets three first tries to achieve a qualifying standard. Those that do will move into the finals on the basis of their best single effort out of three attempts. (Each competitor makes one attempt and then moves to the end of the line in a fixed order.) When possible, the number of finalists in the field events should be comparable to the number of finalists in the track events on the program. In the finals, the best of each competitor's attempts in the competition counts toward determining a winner, including any attempt to break a first-place tie. For example, if a javelin thrower's longest throw is his first one, that will be the one the others need to beat, not his subsequent shorter ones. In nonscratch events (more about these later) all attempts are important since in the case of a tie all of the attempts will be considered in an attempt to break the tie—if the competitors' second-best attempts are equal they will consider their third best and so on until one athlete has a better one.

With a few exceptions (made for athletes who are registered for more than one event), if a competitor misses his turn, he doesn't get a chance to make it up. In the pole vault and high jump, the tardy contestant starts at the height of the bar at the time of arrival. The bar is never lowered for a late contestant.

Athletes should be prompt and businesslike. A competitor sometimes can get permission to take the trials in other than the prearranged order so that he or she can compete in another event. If this means delaying the trials, they must be made up in timely fashion. If there's too much delay, the competitor risks having the trial declared a foul, and a second such delay could get the competitor disbarred from any further trials in that event. The only consolation would be that any performances by that competitor up until then would stand.

Other than in the high jump, where approved markers may be placed, making marks on the runways is not allowed. Competitors may place approved marks alongside it. Competitors may not put any kind of marker or ''target'' in pits, landing areas, or throwing sectors.

Jumping Events

Like many of the other sporting ancestors of today's track and field events, jumping competitions were popular at the local rural athletic events that preceded the national and international organization of sports. Competitive jumping may be older than most: it shows up in woodcuts from the 1500s. During the 1900s, all manner of jump, hop, bound, and somersault was practiced competitively, but as of 1912, the official Olympic events have been the high, long, and triple jumps, and the pole vault. That means that there are no preliminaries. Entrants just compete until they are disqualified.

The high jump and pole vault are scratch events. Each competitor takes a turn in order. A jumper may skip a turn or cease trying after a failure and wait for the bar to be moved up (by predetermined amounts) to the next or any subsequent height. Three consecutive failures to clear the bar, regardless of height, means elimination. During the competition, the jumper may not go back and attempt a lesser height. This leads to a lot of psyching of opponents and strategic timing of jumps.

Unlike the pole vault and high jump, the long and triple jumps are not organized for strategically minded individuals. They consider, rather, the best of a competitor's competitive jumps.

HIGH JUMP

In the early days of high jumping, no official rules existed, nor did soft landing areas. Technique was determined by self-preservation as much as anything. Techniques of bar clearance and run-up varied over the following century. Possibly the most dramatic variation came in the late 1960s when Dick Fosbury invented his famous flop technique, which became practical because of a technological advance, the advent of thick foam landing areas.

In the high jump, the highest jump prior to three failures wins.

High jumpers must leave the ground from one foot.

The ends of the crossbar rest on flat pegs facing each other on the support poles—a touch will send them tumbling. Knocking the bar off the supports is a failure . . .

... and so is touching the ground on the other side of the support poles by jumping under, around, or falling through the support poles for any reason, including an aborted jump attempt.

POLE VAULT

An English athlete named Tom Ray won the United States' pole vaulting title in 1888. He was the last Englishman ever to do so, and much more has changed since then. In those days, vaulters used poles made of ash wood to fling themselves over the bar onto plain ground. Ray's method of winning was to climb the pole hand-over-hand—that technique is now banned. Ash poles have disappeared, replaced in evolutionary stages by bamboo, metal, and fiberglass. Today's pole vaulter also is accustomed to a prepared-surface approach track, a special takeoff trough in which each vaulter is supposed to place the end of the pole for push-off, and to keep the bones intact, a cushioned landing area.

Poles are made of a variety of materials or combination of materials. Any metal surface must be smooth; the pole can be bound by tape, but not more than 2 layers of adhesive tape. The bottom foot of the pole is an exception—it can have many layers of tape. It's all right for vaulters to use their own personal poles and they aren't compelled to let others use them.

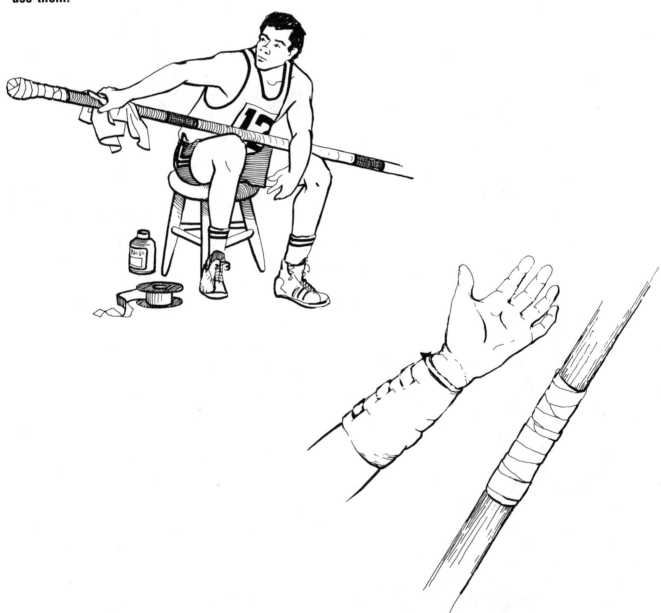

Vaulters may not use gloves. For an improved grip, vaulters may put resin or something similar on their hands or the pole. Tape on the jumper's hands or fingers is okay only to cover a cut.

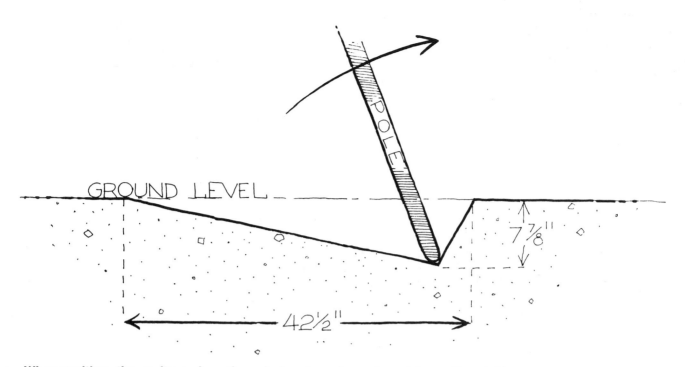

GROUND LEVEL

POLE

7 7/8"

42 1/2"

When vaulting, the vaulters place the pole in a box of wood, metal, or other rigid material sunk even with the ground.

If the meet is using movable equipment, it's okay for the pole vaulter to ask that the distance of the crossbar from the takeoff and landing areas be adjusted. However, it may not be moved more than 15 inches closer to the runway or more than 31 inches closer to the landing zone.

The highest jump prior to three consecutive failures wins. A failed attempt happens in several ways. The most obvious is that the jumper knocks the bar down. The crossbar rests very lightly on the support poles—a touch will dislodge it.

It's also a failure if the jumper touches the ground on the other side of the vertical poles with any part of the body or pole without first clearing the bar.

The jumper's attempt will be a failure if, after leaving the ground, that jumper changes hand positions, either by placing the lower hand above the upper one or moving the upper hand higher on the pole. Finally, if anyone touches the pole and the judge believes that touch stopped the pole from dislodging the bar, it will be counted as a failure.

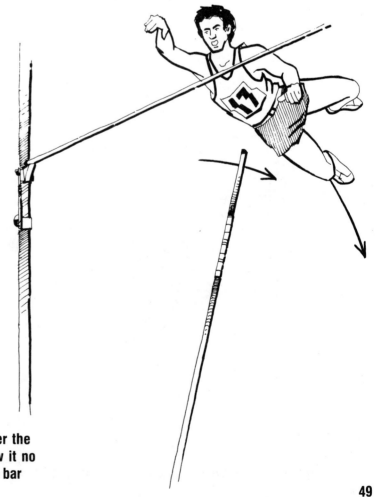

It used to be a failure if the pole passed under the crossbar, but the rules have changed and now it no longer is. The pole may pass under the cross bar and the attempt is still good.

Once a foul was called if the competitor began to vault but stopped short. But the rules have changed and this action is now permissible.

If a jumper's pole breaks in the midst of an attempt, it counts as neither an attempt nor a failure.

LONG JUMP AND TRIPLE JUMP
Long Jump

A year before traveling to Berlin and embarrassing Hitler's ''master race'' in 1936, black American athlete, Jesse Owens, set a record for the long jump—26 feet, 8¼ inches—that was to stand for 25 years.

The long jump is a seemingly simple and elegant feat, but one that can be excelled at by only the best athletes. It consists of an approach run, followed by the farthest possible horizontal leap the jumper can make—the kind of thing Indiana Jones does from boxcar to boxcar in the movies. Yet it is more complicated than it sounds and, like everything described so far in this volume, it is far more difficult than it appears: A long jumper takes a precise number of strides in the approach run—varying among individuals from 20 to 24. It is imperative that they reach the takeoff area on the foot with which they want to push off from the ground, and once there the jumper must put on a huge, precisely timed burst of speed and a powerful lift. All the elegance of a natural impulse: ''Let's see who can jump the farthest.''

Recognized by the IAAF as part of the international program in 1913, the triple jump is just what it sounds like—a jumping competition for distance that allows three jumps. It is performed in a continuous bounding series of leaps. These leaps are often called, in the order in which they are performed, the hop, step, and jump. The longest total distance for the three jumps wins.

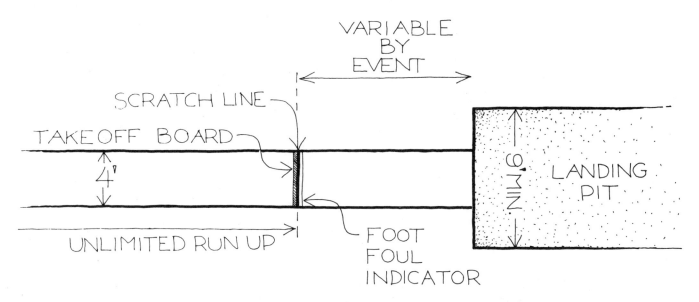

The measurements for the long-jump run-up and landing area are rigidly prescribed.

Technically, the length of the run for a long jump is unlimited. As in all field events, each jumper gets official credit for their best try rather than for their final one. The longest single jump wins.

To record foot faults, there is a tray of soft, oily clay located immediately after the legal takeoff area. The line where the clay begins is called the "scratch line." The jump is measured by the distance between the scratch line and nearest landing mark the jumper makes in the sand. The tape is stretched from the nearest mark in the landing area straight back to form a right angle to the scratch line. If it were stretched from the actual takeoff spot to the actual landing spot—on the diagonal—it would add length to the jump.

It's a failure if the jumper, when jumping, touches the ground and leaves a mark in the clay beyond the scratch line. It's also a foul to take off outside the side edges of the takeoff board, which would make foot faults very difficult to detect. It is okay, however, for the jumper to leave the ground before the takeoff line.

It's a failure if the jumper, when landing, touches the ground outside the landing area in a place that's closer to the takeoff line than the mark in the landing area is. In short, this jumper may not support herself with a hand in the grass to keep her rear end from marking the sand.

Walking back through the landing area after completing the jump is a foul . . .

. . . and it's a foul to perform a somersault.

Triple Jump

In the triple jump, after the first hop, the competitor must land on the same foot as that used for the takeoff; the other foot is used for the second landing; and either or both feet for the final landing. The distance of the takeoff board from the sand depends on the ability of the competitors.

The competitors must be sure not to let their trailing foot scuff the ground, because even though no advantage is gained, the jump will be called a failure. Other than this, the rules are the same as for the running long jump.

Throwing Events

Ancient, medieval, and nineteenth-century sporting games included a variety of throwing events. The rules and the objects thrown evolved over the years, and some objects from older games survive only as mysterious names. It is fairly certain that the basic forms remain the same. The major throwing events conducted today are the hammer, the javelin, the shot put, and the discus.

A throw, like a jump, includes an approach run or a spin for momentum, followed by the competitor propelling into the air, in a prescribed manner, an object of prescribed weight and shape. The ultimate goal is distance: who can fling that thing the farthest. It might therefore seem as if, in throwing competitions, the victor would be determined simply by who is biggest and strongest. If this were true, it certainly wouldn't be much of a "sport." Throwing events do require strength, but skill and technique are also vital, in a similar way that they're vital to a baseball pitcher—fast and hard's not enough. There's a good deal of precision also required.

Throwing events, in part because of the kind of physique demanded by the heavier-weight events, have encountered much controversy in relation to the ingestion of dangerous steroids. Therefore, this is probably a good place to remind young athletes that the use of drugs for enhanced performance is strictly forbidden in all sports.

GENERAL RULES

In throwing events, competitors may use only those implements that are provided by the games committee. In fact, no other implements may even be taken into the arena. If competitors want to use their own implements, they must have them approved beforehand by the committee, but they may not modify them in any way once they've been approved. Also, during the competition the implements aren't considered private property. Using an illegal implement is grounds for disqualification.

Also, no flags or markers may be used by the athletes as targets or goals to mark the landing sectors. In all throwing events, the competitor gets three trials and the longest single throw wins.

In the shot put, hammer throw, discus, and javelin, if the implement fails to fall completely—excluding the hammer's handle and wire—inside the inner edge of the landing sector, then it is a foul throw. In the diagram, A and C are valid. B and D are not.

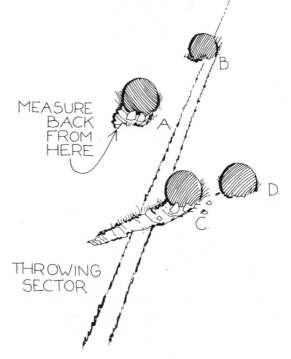

MEASURE BACK FROM HERE

THROWING SECTOR

In all throwing events, the throw must be begun from a stationary position. It's a foul throw if the competitor touches the boundary of the throwing area, or the stop-board, or the ground outside the throwing area after stepping into the area and commencing a throw. It's all right if, during the windup and follow-through, an arm or leg hangs over and outside the edge of the throwing area in the air. It is also a foul if the competitor improperly releases the implement in a throwing attempt.

In throwing events that commence from a circle, competitors may interrupt their own trials—if they do so without committing a foul—put the implement down, exit the rear of the circle, and then recommence the trial.

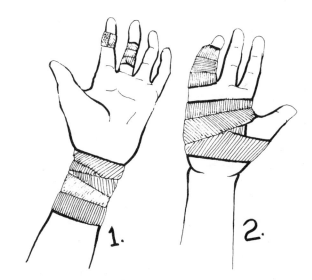

It's okay for hammer throwers to wear special gloves during competition, but other throwers may not.

No device or method—such as taping the fingers together—is allowed to help the competitor make a better throw. Individual fingers may be taped for protection in the hammer, javelin, and shot put, but this tape should be shown to the chief judge for an okay. No other tape is allowed on the hand, except to cover a cut. The wrists, though, may be taped.

Competitors may use substances on their hands to aid the grip. In the picture, hand #1 is okay, but hand #2 isn't.

Competitors aren't supposed to leave the circle until the implement has landed. When it has landed, they should then exit through the rear half of the circle. This athlete's trial will be disallowed because he could not contain his curiosity.

In discus, shot put, javelin, and hammer throw, the measuring tape is stretched from the mark it made to the center of the circle, but the throw is measured by the line between where it first marked the landing area to just inside the circle. In the picture, the judges will measure from A to B, but they will stretch the tape to C.

SHOT PUT

The standard-size shot put, developed in Scotland's Highland Games, stays with us today. The simplicity of the event seems to ensure that the event itself will be handed down generation to generation with few changes. The technique, however, certainly has room for change and innovation, consisting as it does of three parts: the movement forward (the glide); the put position; and the put itself. With certain basic conventions and the rules concerning the throwing, each competitor works out their own style.

The shot is made of solid iron, brass, or some other metal not softer than brass. It has a diameter of at least $4^{11}/_{32}$ inches. The weight is 16 pounds for men and 8 pounds, 13 ounces for women.

The throwing circle is enclosed by a band of steel or wood that is sunk in the ground, level with the surface, and painted white. Inside the circle is hard-packed earth or concrete. For indoor competitions, the circle may be painted on the wood floor. In both cases, the throwing area must measure precisely as shown above. Shot putting is made from a circle with an inside diameter of 7 feet.

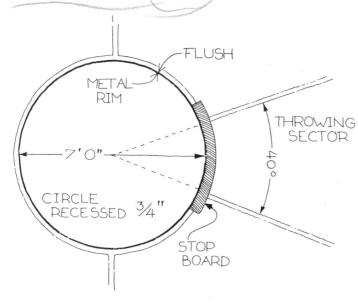

In throwing events that commence from a circle, it's okay to touch the inside of the iron band or stop-board.

The shot is put from the shoulder with only one hand. When the competitor is inside and has taken the stance, he or she should be holding the shot so that it touches or almost touches the chin. After this point, the hand is not supposed to come down until the shot's been flung. And the shot should never be pulled back by the putter so that it goes behind the line of the shoulders.

DISCUS

The discus could logically be compared to a very heavy Frisbee. But because of its weight, throwing the discus is no backyard pastime, and the motions involved in this throwing can't be picked up in a quick five-minute lesson.

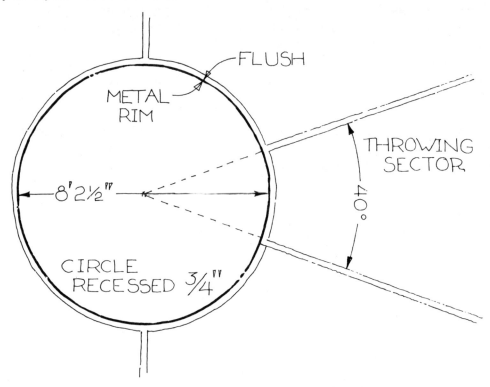

The discus is thrown from a circle constructed along the same lines as the shot put's. The discus circle is larger and has an inside diameter measuring 8 feet, 2½ inches.

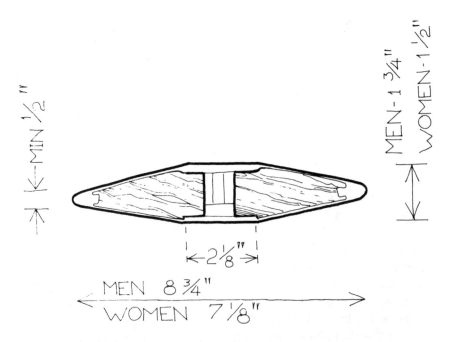

Like other throwing objects, the discus has rigid specifications as detailed in this cross section. It is flat, rigid, made of wood with a metal rim.

JAVELIN

Watching a javelin being thrown by an accomplished athlete is a very evocative sight, perhaps because it is such an obvious throwback to the days of prehistoric hunting and warfare. The javelin could very well just be called a spear, although it is a very specialized sort of spear thrown, in organized sports, in a very specialized sort of way.

The javelin is thrown from a runway that must be at least 98 feet and 6 inches long and must be no longer than 120 feet. The runway is contained within two parallel lines 13 feet, 1½ inches apart. The throw is made from behind a wide arc. The arc is made from a 2¾-inch-wide band of board or metal sunk level into the ground.

In adult competition, the tip of the metal head must strike the ground before any other part of the javelin and the measurement will be made from the mark made by this tip even if the javelin falls back flat on the ground. The measuring tape will be stretched back from the foul line, through the arc, behind which the throws are made and to the center of the imaginary circle on which the arc is drawn. The actual measurement, however, will be only from the first point of the landing to the arc.

This is the end of the javelin run-up and the scratch line. The run-up is 120 feet.

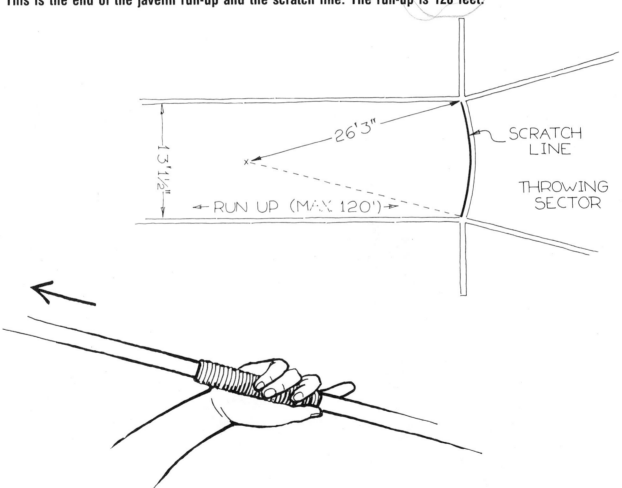

To be valid, the javelin must be thrown by one hand only, with the little finger nearest to the javelin's point and the thrower's last contact with the javelin on the grip. Although the goal is not to impale the javelin in the landing surface, it must strike the ground point-first.

Javelin throwing is a difficult skill to master, so for youth and up to high school level, the measurement will be made from where the first part touches. Also, if the javelin lands flat, the measurement will be made from the cord handle around the middle of the pole.

The thrower may not step on or over the scratch line,
although he or she may, in the follow-through,
lean the upper body over the line.

In throwing the javelin, the athlete must not step over *either* of the parallel lines of the throwing area.

The javelin isn't supposed to be slung or hurled.

HAMMER

The modern hammer bears very little resemblance to the sledge hammers thrown in medieval times. It is a heavy round weight suspended on a wire. At the end of wire is the handle that the athlete grips. It is doubtful that the corpulent Henry VIII, famous for his hammer-throwing prowess, would have much luck today. Nevertheless, the impulse is the same in this highly skilled event. Interestingly, in part because it takes years to develop this skill, hammer throwers will ordinarily be some of the most mature contestants found on the field. These competitors also combine a good deal of grace with hefty proportions; one popular—and quite legal—attire variation practiced by these athletes is the wearing of ballet slippers during competition.

The hammer for today's adult competitor weighs 16 pounds with a diameter of about 5 inches; weights for other class competitions vary.

The grip must be made so that it doesn't stretch as it's thrown. The wire is connected to the head by a swivel, sometimes made with a ball bearing. The total length of the hammer is around 4 feet.

The hammer thrower in the starting position before preliminary swings may rest the hammer's head on the ground either inside or outside the circle.

It's not foul if the hammer's head touches the ground during the preliminary swings or turns—but if it touches the ground during these swings and the thrower halts and begins again, that is a foul.

THROWING
SECTOR

As in all throwing events, valid throws must fall within the marked landing sector but the handle of the hammer does not count and may land outside.

A Special Note about Ties in Field Events

Ties in high jump and pole vault: The athlete with the lowest number of jumps needed to clear the height where the tie occurs is awarded the higher place; if it's still a tie, then the one with the lowest number of failures overall in the competition is the winner. If it's *still* a tie, here's what happens: If the tie is not over first place, the competitors will have equal standing. If the tie has to do with first place, the tying competitors have one more jump at just higher than the tying height. Then the bar will be continually lowered or raised until someone has a better jump and the tie is decided.

Ties in field events determined by distance: In these cases, the second-best or third-best performance in that competition by those who are tied will determine the winner. If they've tied all the way down the line, then they'll make a new try till the tie's decided.

COMBINED EVENTS

Privately sponsored combination competitions—decathlons and so forth—have soared in popularity in recent years, offering a stimulating challenge for the physically fit.

Though the Greeks had similar events, there's little evidence that they were considered as important as single events—the guiding principle stays with us, however, and that is as a test of all-around athletic ability, rather than a single honed skill.

Over the years, myriad combinations have been and are still being experimented and tried. These include, for men and women, indoor and outdoor: pentathlon, decathlon, heptathlon, all-around competitions, weight events, and experimental events. All these include some combination of hurdles, running, jumping, and throwing efforts. In the Olympics and most organized track and field competitions, however, the main combined events are the men's decathlon and the women's heptathlon. Indoor combined events are usually pentathlon for both men and women.

The men's decathlon, extending over two days, runs its events in this order:

First day: 100-meter dash, long jump, shot put, high jump, 400-meter dash.

Second day: 110-meter hurdles, discus throw, pole vault, javelin throw, 1500-meter run.

The men's indoor pentathlon includes the long jump, the 60-meter hurdles, the shot put, the high jump, and the 1000-meter run in that order. This represents a good mix of events, because the athletes don't use the same skills or muscle groups in consecutive events: javelin throw, 200-meter dash, the discus, and the 1500-meter run.

The seven events of the women's heptathlon are held in two days, in this order:

First day: 100-meter hurdles, high jump, shot put, and 200-meter run.

Second day: long jump, javelin, and 800-meter run.

The only variation from this for indoor pentathlons for women is that instead of 1000-meter runs, they run an 800-meter race.

The general track and field rules for individual events also apply to multi-event competitions, with a few procedural differences, primarily the number of attempts allowed. One important thing to know is that if an athlete is disqualified from an event for fouling a competitor, the disqualified athlete can compete in the remaining events unless the referee rules otherwise.

The competitor that wins will be the one who scores the most total points in all events, which are awarded according to special scoring tables.

Younger competitors as well as adults participate in combined events. The bantams have a triathlon that includes the 100-meter dash, the high jump, the shot put with a special lightweight shot.

The midgets and juniors participate in pentathlons that include hurdles, long jump, shot put, high jump, and an 800-meter run. The multi-event competitions for the other groups are the same as for adults.

TEAM COMPETITION

Obviously an athlete isn't going to be turning in a solo performance on the relay race. The fact that an event can be competed in by individuals or by a member of the team makes it very attractive. Overall team competition is another way to achieve cooperation in track and field athletics. Team members can contribute to a common point total, adding interest to a meet as a whole, and they may be inspired to excel by the support and encouragement of their teammates.

The events on the program listed for team competition are scored by points as follows:

10 points for each first place scored;
8 for each second;
6 for each third;
4 for each fourth;
2 for each fifth;
and 1 for each sixth.

For smaller regional events, the scoring is:

5 for each first place;
3 for each second;
2 for each third;
and 1 for each fourth.

In team running competitions such as long-distance, cross-country, or race-walking events, the scoring is as follows: A team's score comes from the combined time of the scoring members—the lowest combined time wins. When teams are incomplete because not enough runners finish a race, due to injury or exhaustion, for example, individual times are still eligible for awards. But the times of runners in incomplete teams and individual runners don't count toward team scores.

OFFICIALS

On first sight, the number and variety of track and field officials may seem staggering, and for good reason. It is no exaggeration to say that a track and field competition has more officials than any other sporting event. Yet there's a good and logical reason for this state of affairs. Namely, numerous events actually are being conducted simultaneously, so there is no way the handful of officials in, for instance, a basketball game would be enough for a track and field meet. In addition, many of the events cover large distances and a platoon of officials is necessary to make sure the action is being thoroughly overseen. These include not only the people described in some detail below, but implement inspectors, juries of appeal, finish-line coordinators, and more. All of these folks have worked hard to become certified officials. It is only through their efforts and the work of other support personnel— announcers, surveyors, press stewards, and doctors—that these complex, labor-intensive events are ever held.

It's the referee's job to enforce all rules and decisions, and also to decide questions of how a meet should be conducted in any way that's not set down in the rules.

The referee is there to warn competitors about improper conduct and to exclude them from competition if necessary. The simplest way to get disqualified from the rest of the meet is to refuse to obey an official, to be unsporting, or to use offensive language or gestures. Not only will that get a competitor barred from the rest of the meet's events, the referee can make a detailed statement to the registration committee, who may then take further action.

The fellow above is making a protest regarding the judgment of an official; this sort of protest is never recognized. If any other protest is going to be made to the referee about something that happened during an event, it must be made within 30 minutes after the results are announced. For road races, however, the time limit is 24 hours. The games committee or referee may request that the protest be made verbally or in writing. For national championships, protests *must* be made in writing. The referee or committee should decide protests immediately if they possibly can. If it is necessary for more evidence or testimony to be gathered, the competitors may continue competing in the meantime. Track and field events being held simultaneously should have separate head judges, but there is only one head referee for the entire meet.

The referee supervises the chief inspector, who in turn supervises the inspectors. It's up to the chief inspector to position the inspectors where they can best do their jobs. Once the chief tells an inspector where to work, that inspector takes the position and carefully watches the competition. The inspectors are positioned and assigned to supervise such things as the conduct of hurdle races and the passing of batons in relay events. At the sight of a foul or rule violation, the inspector waves a red flag and tells the chief—in writing, if requested—exactly what took place. In race walking, technique rules are the responsibility of the walking judges. Inspectors don't have the power to make those decisions.

The starter and recall starter occupy prominent positions in track officiating. Once the competitors are at the mark, the starter in charge is the only one to judge whether any competitor has made a false start. If the starter has an assistant or recall starter helping, they too can recall the competitors if they believe the start wasn't fair. Only the starter, however, may make a warning or disqualification. TAC recommends that events with a staggered start have at least two recall starters.

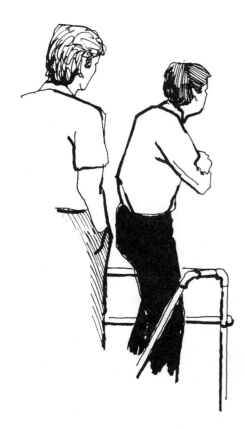

There should be at least four judges at the finish line, one of whom is the chief. These judges should stand at least 16 feet away and in line with the finish line; when at all possible it's best for them to stand on an elevated platform.

When the judges announce the order that the competitors finished, that's final unless an appeal to a photo-finish panel is made with, as evidence, the photograph of an approved photographic device.

If an approved device is being used to photograph the finish, a photo-finish panel is designated to review the resulting image.

Two methods of timing are official: hand timing and fully automatic timing. Hand timing can be done either with stopwatches or electric digital watches.

The games committee designates a chief timer for every meet. This chief oversees all aspects of timing, including assigning timers, supervising time recording, being familiar with the records of the events so as to know if one's been broken, and if there is a record, to inspect the timing device and make sure that timer signs the record application.

When finish times are recorded by a fully automatic device, timekeepers are still needed—they must record what the device has determined as the finish time. Automatic timing should be used whenever practical, and the times recorded will be the official times unless the referee determines that the device wasn't working properly; then the hand times will be official. It is interesting to note that .05 second is added to fully automatic timing results—which represents the equivalent of the reaction time of a human timer to the starting gun.

It's up to the chief field judge to make sure that all equipment, landing zones, and other areas of the event conform to the rules of The Athletic Congress. The chief judge should not be assigned so much to do, however, that it's impossible to judge the performance of the competitors. The judging includes measuring and recording each trial made of each competitor in any event. For the record, the measurements are gathered from all the judges.

In the long and triple jumps and throwing events, the judge indicates a valid trial by raising a white flag. A red flag indicates a nonvalid performance.

For each event, the scorer collects the results, the times, heights, distances, wind-gauge information, and photo-finish pictures from the judges and timers and passes the information on to the announcer and to the meet director.

The clerk of the course will have the names and numbers of the competitors and will notify them when it's time to go to the starting point. When the competitors in an event are being handicapped at different marks because they are mismatched, the clerk places each competitor at the proper place and watches to see that they stay there until the "get ready."

The wind-gauge operator takes and records the wind velocity in the direction of running for distances of 220 yards and less and the long and triple jumps. The operator turns these measurements over to the scorer and the referee. A wind speed of 2 meters per second can nullify an apparent record.

The marshal is a member of the support staff. He or she is in charge of the enclosed competition area, which should be occupied only by competitors and officials. He also may have assistants, which he assigns to particular areas.

RECORDS

Don't bother writing the games committee for that world record you broke in your 6 A.M. training. Like golf's unobserved hole-in-one, no performance, no matter how amazing, is valid for a record outside the arena of official competition.

A record performance must be approved by the appropriate committees, including the national governing body.

Learn the rules for all your favorite sports with Perigee's popular *Sports Rules in Pictures* series!

Illustrated throughout with clearly captioned, easy-to-follow drawings of actual playing situations, these handy guides to the rules of America's favorite sports are ideal for players, weekend athletes, and fans alike. For the last word on any dispute, these guides will provide the answer.

Baseball Rules in Pictures
By G. Jacobs and J. R. McCrory
This ready guide is a quick and easy way to learn baseball rules and check decisions. Nearly 200 captioned drawings cover sections on pitching, batting, baserunning, and fielding. Included is a foreword by legendary umpire Ron Luciano and the complete Official Rules of Baseball.

Official Little League Baseball ® Rules in Pictures
Introduction by Dr. Creighton J. Hale,
President, Little League Baseball
Incorporating more than 150 illustrations, the full text of Little League's Official Playing Rules, and all the latest rule changes, this straightforward guide is an indispensable handbook for the two million youngsters who play Little League baseball every year. Parents, coaches, managers, and umpires will find the book an essential companion on the field or in the stands.

Softball Rules in Pictures
By G. Jacobs McCrory
Revised by Michael J. Brown
Over 90 all-new drawings and a new, easy-to-follow text clarify the latest rules from the Amateur Softball Association of America in chapters on equipment, pitching, batting, and baserunning. The complete text of the rules is included along with umpire signals to help players and spectators follow the game more easily.

Football Rules in Pictures
Edited by Don Schiffer and Lud Duroska
Both stadium and armchair football fans will welcome this newly revised handbook including the latest Official National Football League Digest of Rules with its Summary of Penalties, pro, college, and high school interpretations of the game rules, and quick-reference guide to officials' signals.

Basketball Rules in Pictures
Edited by A. G. Jacobs
Profuse illustrations, captions, and text provide a complete explanation of the essential regulations of basketball, followed by a section on basic basketball play and patterns and a helpful guide to officials' signals.

Hockey Rules in Pictures
By The National Hockey League
Incorporating the complete text of the NHL Official Rules Book and the latest rule changes in use today, this handy book clearly and carefully explains goals and scoring, face-offs, high-sticking, board-checking, falling on the puck, and more. Includes a quick-reference guide to officials' signals.

Amateur Wrestling Rules in Pictures
By Michael Brown
With its hundreds of different techniques, wrestling is one of the most demanding and complicated sports to understand. With helpful stop-action illustrations and easy-to-read language, this practical guide explains wrestling's international rules, weight classes, officials' signals, boundary regulations, scoring, and much more.

Volleyball Rules in Pictures
By Michael Brown
Here is the first fully illustrated guide to America's fastest-growing sport, featuring the complete text of the Official United States Volleyball Rules as approved by the U.S. Volleyball Association, a handy guide to officials' hand signals, and over 150 line drawings and captions that explain every aspect of the game.

Golf Rules in Pictures
An Official Publication of the United States Golf Association
Introduction by Arnold Palmer
Scores of clearly captioned pictures cover golf rules from hazards, penalty strokes, and scoring to the number of clubs allowed and what to do when you accidentally hit an opponent's ball. Included is the complete text of The Rules of Golf as approved by the U.S. Golf Association and the Royal and Ancient Golf Club of St. Andrews, Scotland.

Tennis Rules and Techniques in Pictures
By Michael J. Brown
This authoritative guide explains and illustrates the rules of tennis—including doubles play—and describes the basic techniques of tennis, providing instructions on the various grips and service and advice on court tactics. The complete text of the official rules of the United States Tennis Association is included.

Ordering *Sports Rules in Pictures* is easy and convenient. Just call 1-800-631-8571 or send your order to:
The Putnam Publishing Group
390 Murray Hill Parkway, Dept. B
East Rutherford, NJ 07073
Also available at your local bookstore or wherever paperbacks are sold.

			PRICE	
			U.S.	CANADA
✓	Baseball Rules in Pictures	399-51129	$6.95	$ 9.25
	Official Little League Baseball® Rules in Pictures	399-51531	6.95	9.25
✓	Softball Rules in Pictures	399-51356	6.95	9.25
✓	Football Rules in Pictures	399-51479	6.95	9.25
✓	Basketball Rules in Pictures	399-51590	7.95	10.50
	Hockey Rules in Pictures	399-51480	7.95	10.50
	Amateur Wrestling Rules in Pictures	399-51589	7.95	10.50
	Volleyball Rules in Pictures	399-51537	6.95	9.25
	Golf Rules in Pictures	399-51438	6.95	9.25
	Tennis Rules and Techniques in Pictures	399-51405	6.95	9.25

Subtotal $_____

*Postage & Handling $_____

Sales Tax $_____
(CA, NJ, NY, PA)

Total Amount Due $_____
Payable in U.S. Funds
(No cash orders accepted)

*Postage & Handling: $1.00 for 1 book, 25¢ for each additional book up to a maximum of $3.50.

Please send me the titles I've checked above. Enclosed is my:

☐ check   ☐ money order

Please charge my

☐ Visa   ☐ MasterCard

Card # _____ Expiration date _____

Signature as on charge card _____

Name _____

Address _____

City _____ State _____ Zip _____

Please allow six weeks for delivery. Prices subject to change without notice.